CW00847909

Dark Days

Dark Days

An Anthology

Chris Botragyi

Copyright (C) 2020 Chris Botragyi
Layout design and Copyright (C) 2020 Next Chapter
Published 2020 by Magnum Opus – A Next Chapter Imprint
This book is a work of fiction. Names, characters, places, and incidents are the product
of the author's imagination or are used fictitiously. Any resemblance to actual events,
locales, or persons, living or dead, is purely coincidental.
All rights reserved. No part of this book may be reproduced or transmitted in any form
or by any means, electronic or mechanical, including photocopying, recording, or by
any information storage and retrieval system, without the author's permission.

Contents

A Frintonian View

The contours of the pebbles hurts my feet as I tiptoe over the golden sand
The salty breeze teases me emphatically, playfully, as cool water swirls around
my swishing hand
Tennis balls bounce fast as wet dogs pant heavily, happy at pleasing their own-
ers
Squinting eyes cast far out over the blocks of foamy water, chopping hard as
I stand firm
Ever the romantic loner
I walk slowly, quietly playing tag with the rushing tide, recalling memories of
a once happy youth
The sun's warm glare shines bright, reflecting, guides me towards a broken
shark's tooth
I brush crystallised grains from the serrated cutter, wondering what else is
buried deep
In the blue cemetery
Carefree children run wild, stealing pleasure from throwing a plastic disc
As they stuff their faces with confectionary
Vibrant beach huts stand to attention like wooden soldiers, alive as colourful
lipstick pouts
I smile to myself... this is what Frinton-on-sea is all about.

Achilles—The Myrmidon Terror of Troy

Today, Achilles paints revenge upon the fleshy mask he adorns
His worn terrain peeks thoughtfully through the slivers of slippage,
Radiating a pugnacious incandescence, that feeds off the stinging air,
Itself lovingly bleeding life from the charcoal lungs of Patroclus

For as the crows scour King Priam's gentle, affluent pastures... Squawking
their death cry
Picking at the leftover riches of poverty-stricken soldiers' skulls, that still bear
bronze helmets
For the sun's blazing reflection singes hopping black feathers
That desecrate courageous flesh, dismantling therein the golden sands of time-
lessness,
Before mortality
Stains the seas red; it snakes down Poseidon's salty windpipe, leaving him
drunk on
Mortal juice that froths with war
Hatred hugs the sides of the bobbing, creaking Archaean Biremes,
Staining, like wine and bread congealed stubbornly to the wooden plate.

Achilles' fierce tongue has tasted King Agamemnon's true heart
The taste soured!
Weeping, yearning and aching for Patroclus,
The enmity streaks through heartbroken veins
Racing headstrong as Xanthas and Balios,
The flow of poison flames within, burning for retribution against the mighty Hector
Fantasising Achilles dreams of Archaean steel swiftly carrying the Prince of Troy away
To the underworld in a glorious golden chariot of death,
Crafted and nurtured for the occasion by Athena herself

The war-cry trembles the very foundations of Olympus,
Toppling the gods from their cloudy thrones
Briseis begs for the fury to break, but
Myrmidon loyalty hungers—craves—for their master's charge
But Achilles, Son of Peleus, fires them back...
This fight is his to be immortalised in the dust-filled grounds of Troy
Agamemnon smiles sweetly... Patroclus' fall has saved this war!

Achilles and Hector dance the warriors dance
Each fanning their plumage in an ostentatious vanity and strength
Pirouetting, like crazed marionettes to the gods' masterful puppeteers,
Before deciding Achilles is due his glory and immortality in the annals of history,
All for the impertinent wrongs against him done by wicked Agamemnon

With a flash of greaves and swift thrust of blade
Hector wilts in the glaring sun
His Trojan soul empties with a spewing of claret mortality that
Bubbles in the fine, dry soil...
Achilles stands proud and tall, his handsome face adored by the gods
Uniting in a Greek battle-cry that thunders the bloody air, consuming all of Troy.

All at Sea

Staring out to sea, choppy waters cut like glimmering meat cleavers
Yellow rays claw viciously as they fight the heavy cement clouds
Desperate to shine a light
Whipped up breeze attacks contorted, line-riddled face as lids close
To protect lifeless dark eyes
Putrid salty smell crawls up the nasal canal like a mountain climber
Digging his crampons in as he hikes his way to the top
Nauseating feeling, deep breaths through gritted teeth
As beating heart fuels stinging emotions
Soul lost at sea in a flood of sharp, slicing memories, forever floating alone
Until the day comes when the weighted burden will drown the spirit
Numb hands grip the cold steel barrier
The shiver shooting through the body like an electrical current
Seagull's squawk slices throbbing grey matter, a hot knife through butter
Head falls in defeat, mind scrambled in a tangled web
As pain wafts in, finger over its lips, shushing all as it creeps closer
Invading, engulfing, it swarms around
As a mother wrapping her child tightly in a warm blanket
Life swamped in thick sludge, helpless like a fly stuck in treacle
It is too much, it is too much grief and effort to keep fighting
Can end the conflict now, it'll be over in minutes if that is what's required
One last battle, that's all is ever said, now compose oneself
There's an internal war to be won.

Black Heart to Fresh Start

The trees are lonely, whispering silently
Eyes around are the windows to your soul
Burning deep as you cry defiantly
Helpless in the haze, like a newborn foal
Charcoaled heart buried deep beneath the snow
Inner peace shattered, venomous snake bites
Ungovernable rage, boiling blood flows
Poison walks stinging veins, to man's delight
Branching out to your deep blackened roots
Gripping the tunnel of life by the throat
Aching desires fuel evil salutes
Man's propensity forces Devil's gloat
As your dishonest discrepancy fails
God laughs as your quisling faces curtail.

Christmas Eve

As the realms of fantasy and reality collide
Magic is once again with us inside
As every man tries hard to deny
The excited feelings that make him fly
Along rooftops, skimming the tiles he goes
Brushing and kicking up the crisp white snow
Delivering presents to all kids alike
From teddy bears to dolls to brand new bikes
Squeezing into chimneys all over the world
Laughing and smiling until his beard is all curled
Climbing back up still full of cheer
His job is now done for another year.

Come Midnight

Tick tock tick tock, the pendulum swings bright
As children of all ages gaze into the light
With one eye open when both should be shut
They wait excitedly for the black booted strut
As midnight approaches, along with the snow
He lands in your living room with only one place to go
Soot from the chimney scattered evenly wide
He crouches unsuspectingly, laying parcels with pride
After emptying his sack and filling your stocking
He takes a welcome break in a wooden chair that's rocking
And after tucking into mince pies and a glass of sherry
He vanishes without a trace, leaving all things merry
Children now fast asleep know they came ever so near
To seeing Father Christmas, oh well, they'll have to wait till next year.

Creeping Shadows

Devil's moll smiles innocently and sly
Disappointments anger the brittle mind
While cursing your soul with her evil eye
Ready to snap out of the ties that bind
Old newspapers dance up desolate streets
Her essence lurid, she waits patiently
The breeze and the fog making them obsolete
Out of the shadows lunging violently
Sensing you thrive on the blood of stray hounds
Burning your veins with her pearl bladed fangs
Injecting pure evil as withered heart drowns
Eternal poison flows in crushing pangs
Stolen soul conflates with charcoaled rebirth
Innocence lost, feeding on blood soaked earth.

Crocodile Smile

The bitterness rides in angry waves as the sweltering heat hammers down from the golden globe,
Suspended gracefully in the clear blue sky
Warm drops of dirty sweat roll sadistically down the cracks and terrain of a twisted face
As the reptile within slowly moves, consuming all like a twister moving from town to town
Seeking a feed
Stinging eyes cast out a line, reeling in nothing but dry, desolate land as tiny scavengers scuttle
Across the dusty road
A rough hand climbs the air as it attempts to shield burning skin from the ever glowing gold
That threatens contorted, weary features
Rattlesnakes hiss aggressively as they stare at their cousins, whom are worn lovingly
Over heavy boots, the texture smooth as crystallised grains of sand
Jump back and forth, trying to distance themselves from the danger
Dark shadow cast menacingly as the thick smell of burning rubber conjoins with hazy cigarette
Smoke, dancing together as they invent their own united stench that sickens the atmosphere
Cigarette butt discarded, flying through the air as an amber boulder flung from an ancient catapult,

Ash scattering as it crashes to the road

Aching, sweaty leather boot ends the butt's life, crushing it harshly with a swivel of solid

Black heel as the grinding goes deeper

Stained cowboy hat floats off lank wet hair, shirt sleeve whips across deep-lined forehead

Before the tired hat is put back in its rightful place

Cautionary eyes peek up from under grimy brim as they spy the female equivalent of himself

Standing on the side of the road as her smooth legs glisten in the sunlight

Bright red lipstick draws hard on the brown filter as the smoke sways gently upwards

Framing her feminine features to perfection

Soulless black eyes stare deep at her crocodile skin boots, a wry thick stubbled smile

Climbs her tanned slender legs to her torn, cut off denim shorts

Before saturating the rest of her body in lustful stares, greedily drinking in her raw beauty

An eyebrow raised, ice cold blue eyes look approvingly at the curled lip and

Empty eyes that hide beneath the flailing hat

A shock of cropped peroxide hair, the black rooted splinters rising

Smile casually as the red stained cigarette butt leaves her full, weather beaten lips before

Dropping to the dead earth, another creature of habit as short spiked heel obliterates the glow

Elbows sore from leaning against a rusty signpost as the cowboy moves in for the line

With a grubby nailed tip of the brim, dead eyes stare at her sweat-matted grey crop top,

Half torn that barely covers her tanned, butterfly tattooed midriff

The line flows in a dry husky nicotine ravaged voice as the smile moves in closer

She smiles achingly back as her black painted fingernails creep slowly up his back

Like a spider, placing cold metal against his slippery temple

Both grins travel downwards as eyes wake up

BANG!

Heavy corpse collapses as the vultures eagerly begin to circle, hungry for the pickings
The red pool swims out over the dirty road, thickening quickly as it joins the grit
The smoking gun is placed casually in its leather holster home that occupies frayed denim shorts
Loose cash and cigarettes the only bounty as bright eyes nervously glance left, then right
A wry smile burns down upon the cowboy hat, and what is left inside of it before sleek legs
Stride confidently off to the next stop.

Dark Days

The dark skies congregate hard as the grey moth flaps its wings desperately
Clearing the oppressive thick air, that smothers the innocent like a choking fog
The weary citizen holds his dirty white flag, waving it gingerly from side to side
As he surrenders to the demise of his fallen homeland

Crumpled, tear stained cheeks—exhausted from the war of justice
Drop heavily as screaming violence prevails in a non-moral society
Bloodshot eyes crawl along the grubby path, seeking a shining light
That will propel hope back through the darkness like a shooting star

The muddy foot of corrupted humanity grins sadistically
As it closes down upon the law abiding hand,
Crushing it hard as bloodied fingers extend outwards
Desperate for someone—anyone—to take a stand

Hatred stampedes over the lush green pastures
Celebrating the death of the Scales of Justice
That lay alone, half buried in the earth, broken and forgotten
Sorrowed eyes look to the heavens, silently praying for answers

The soul eaters of modern man take no prisoners,
As in revenge at a bad hand dealt by a cruel life
The deep scar drawn in the sand is stepped over menacingly
Grinning at whoever stands in their way as they live to engage in conflict

Heroes leave the war; on their way home, wait for a welcome that never comes
Only to be forced head first into another battle for social survival
Ordinary man turns a blind eye to the savage, averting his gaze as though
His life depends on it, maybe it does as he opts for selfish safety
Is he to blame?

The dry earth gulps down the cool grey rain that falls from the thundery skies
Drowning the future as it swallows the dreams of a tired generation
Job vacancy: Powerful hands are required to rip England by the scruff of the neck
Pulling it monstrously from the plummeting depths of despair and failure
Please apply within...

The time has come for the man to take charge, and lead the broken land
Into the dawn of a new era
A leader with teeth that is needed to bite the lawless
With a fire that burns ferociously, yet passionately

Blood will be shed, souls will be drained, tears for the innocent will be wept
But we must prevail now, otherwise the next generation—and the country—
May never rise again.
Dead Man Walking
Darkness crawls closer, icy chill threatens
A shivery breath, whispering shotgun
Son of Sam, eloquent insane cretins
Seeking to emasculate, unhinged fun
Its evil peaking in culmination
Screaming black rage, Devil's elitism
Teased trigger fulminates condemnation
Deranged tears run from king's egotism
Crying blood roams elegantly and free
Field of dreams, meticulous corpse wrapping
Like tattooed clown smiling confidently
Ghostly reminders resound in clapping
Charcoal shadows reminiscent of night
Soul disintegrates, flies towards the light.

Egg Head

The shape of an egg—oval, expressionless
A featureless face, blank, like an expert poker player's
Empty, though its pale complexion speaks a thousand words
Its shell, fragile in its expected job of self preservation
That can crack at anytime, weeping its yolky tears
That seep through its splintered psyche, like sticky make-up from yellow mascara lined eyes
The thick tears dribbling cruelly, violently, from its smashed in skull
An angry miniature volcanic eruption of hot gooey chaos
Fragments of a short life lived, litter the beige china like a rubbish strewn beach
But these shells are deaf when put to the ear, no sound of crashing waves here
Bread soldiers ordered to exercise, dive crudely into the steaming pool
White rubbery brain matter scooped out in a spoon-styled lobotomy
The soul is gone, flown
All that remains is an empty shell of an empty shell
Life, it is what it is.

Great is the State of Britain

Mindless violence corrupts impressionable young souls
Sucking blood, choking life for the 'cause'
Don't care about the fall out, just collecting their dole
Hmmm, you looked at me wrong, I think I'll bypass this country's laws
Weak system spits insult to victims' injury
Men with power claim to be powerless to protect?
Dismiss these 'do gooders' for old fashioned gallantry!
Are there any zero tolerant kings whom we can elect?
Sorry, prisons are full, pass go, collect £200 and go home!
I know, we won't build new prisons
We'll waste £400m on another pointless millennium dome!
Hyena thugs cackle at distraught family trees
The devastation branching out from mother to brother to me
The Government's answer? Let's cut more police jobs on the street!
I know, it's easy to look in and pour scorn
But no one will be around for the Prime Ministers meet and greet
See the path this country has taken, look out, to survive do we conform?

Great? Britain

Grim reaper rages at death in the night
His hooded soldiers clamour as they leer
Fires churning everlasting delight

Seeking, destroying, pure evil's in sight
Growing stronger and absorbing mans fear
Grim reaper rages at death in the night

He swings his sickle to end your bright light
As screams of writhing agony are clear
Fires churning everlasting delight

As flames burn eternal, demons take flight
Descending on Earth their time is now here
Grim reaper rages at death in the night

Like desperadoes, won't give up the fight
Hiding behind black clouds as they draw near
Fires churning everlasting delight

Angry youth in revenge, ready to bite
Aligning Hell's troopers as they cohere
Grim reaper rages at death in the night
Fires churning everlasting delight.

I, Alone

Worm infested grave tickles restless old bones
Aching for a comfort blanket of humanity to keep warm
Eternity to ponder where he went wrong, alone
Buzzing ground, hot underneath, the swell rising as an angry swarm
The burning sting, like a thousand poisonous arrow tips
Jolting decrepit leftovers into a dancing lunatic
Skinless hands tear through wood and earth like a devastating tide rip
The pain that lies ahead, adoringly apocalyptic
Vines grip tight, coiling like inquisitive snakes
Split skull rages in the darkness of night
Sobbing now at a wasted life, too late to shed the tag 'reprobate'
The chilling sound forcing tree life to jump and take flight
Lord of the underworld stares into his soulless sockets
Crushing vice hold on neck bone, breathing fiery breath
The scorching flames open up his skeleton like a silver heart-shaped locket
The price paid in Hell? He gets to suffer over and over again, his own violent death.

I, Hypocrite

I want world peace and the end of starvation, yet I want to see the world burn
Wiping the slate clean, putting an end to all things bad
I want the justice system to punish the evil, yet I want to execute them myself
But I am afraid it will make me the same
I strive to be my own man—an individual, yet find myself conforming to gain
a quiet life
Tired of explaining things to others that don't understand
I hate gossips, yet I do so myself to be socially accepted and to fit in
Angry at myself for being so easily led and fake
The quiet life I seek I sometimes have, but most times wish it was noisy and
filled with lively things
I don't drink much or smoke anymore as it's not good for you, yet I crave them,
Missing their comforting friendship as the guilt at wanting them crushes me
I don't care if people don't like me, but I don't understand it if they don't
I want to be loved for who I am, married with children, wanting to change
But the thought of such a change in my life reminds me I'm better off alone

I dream of achieving good things, but the reality of getting there forces me to abandon those dreams
I spend money happily on myself, yet the idea of spending the same amount on someone else
Causes purse strings to be cut
I moan at how selfish and greedy others can be, shaking my head in anger
Yet can't see it when I act the same, mad at the pot and kettle accusations that are pointed
Towards me
I'd love my old raucous teenage life back, but sleep heavily as I'm too tired and lazy
To do anything about it
I wear a crucifix around my neck as a sign of faith, yet often question whether such things
Really do exist
I get impatient at people who can't make simple decisions, yet I struggle to make
The simplest decisions, turning every one into a pros and cons analysis
I seethe at people who are rude and ignorant, yet act the same towards the people who
Care the most about me
I feel depressed and suicidal, yet I see the light at the end of the tunnel
But I don't walk the short walk to reach it
I don't cry as I see it as weakness, yet a sad scene in a movie will cause me to shed a tear
I feel incapable of love, yet I love my pets with a big heart
I tell people to never look back, to have no regrets, yet I'm stuck in the past,
Regretting most of my decisions as I look far back
I do try to be the good in a world full of bad as this is who I really want to be
But it feels like a heavy mask, a mask that's beginning to slip
So does all this make me a hypocrite, or am I simply just being human?

Insomnia of an Angel

For all eternity, I lay awake
Asking why? It wasn't my time to die
The bright white paradise, a tranquil lake

Can't hide my venomous, poisonous snake
That coils hatred in my wings as I fly
For all eternity, I lay awake

Grieving for myself as my body aches
I scour the earth in search of other cries
The bright white paradise, a tranquil lake

That will hold me tight, no more will I shake
I shouldn't be here, you're telling me lies
For all eternity, I lay awake

This can't be real it must be a mistake
But the voice has spoken I must comply
The bright white paradise, a tranquil lake

It's pointless counting sheep, this I can't take
But one thing's for sure, I can never die
For all eternity, I lay awake
The bright white paradise, a tranquil lake

Is Life My Friend?

A lifetime of pain and sorrow, carved elegantly into my hard, granite-skinned
face
Staring through the windows of a broken soul, gazing forlornly
As the sparrows climb high
Eyes narrowed tight, a sharp intake of breath—head turning in fake disgust
As the brief taste of light threatens the icy prison that encases my heart

Balls of ruffled grey feathers dance eloquently in flight
The display pulls on rusty heartstrings, like a subservient violin maestro as
Worn hand shield my wounded face
Bandaging it from the memories of a once warm life, now lost
A short melodious goodbye accompanies feathery travels to pastures new...
My weeping soul aches as it mourns the death of a sixty second friendship

White plastic bag, damaged, released from its contract
Whispers sadly as it weaves through the oppressive air, playing tag with the
breeze
It clings lovingly to my slender torso, embracing it as a coiling snake
Loyal to the end; is this the start of a new friendship?
No.

The quiet, gentle wind teases... is it staying or is it leaving?
Suffocating panic screams hard as emptiness replaces the vacant bag
Desperate fingers reaching out, clawing as my fading smile watches helplessly
As it walks the stairway of air, off on its melancholic purpose

A single tear descends, tickling the mountainous crevices of my rocky face
Zig-zagging down slope as it approaches its suicide leap from chin valley
The full dose of rejection, injected bitterly into the splintered psyche
Forces deflated ego to exhale harshly
A glance to the upside down ocean to ask a question
The suns rays beam powerfully, like scorching tyre marks
The light responds with a car crashing, eye stinging answer

It is said that we hurt the ones we love the most, so you, the pain, are you my friend?
You always hurt me, but you never leave me
Does this mean that you love me eternally?
Anguished heart rumbles as the teary stream begins to ripple, trickle
Changing course with every twitch of oncoming emotion
The icy prison melts slowly, drowning its shivering occupant
Like a silent assassin

Leathery fists clenched for the white knuckle ride
Can't take it anymore, can't breathe, please don't kill me now
I've just found you, my friend.

Our Father, Refugee, Orphan

Our Father, who art in Heaven
Are you tired from the billions of years of creation?
Now resting with your head in your hands as you endure
The pain that thunders evermore
Staring on with embarrassment and shame
Realising that your efforts have been wasted
Lost in a desperation amidst the murky blanket of stars
"Ah, but there is good amongst the rotting core," I hear you preach
As you deliberately twiddle your finger in the oceans
Yes, oh righteous one
But who are you trying to convince?
Unable to live with the guilt
It is only you who seeks to justify one's own actions

Methinks you are bored and need another hobby
Either that or you do indeed despise your handiwork
But wait... Did you not create us in your own image?
Then sadly you are the cause and the effect, my friend!
This is why you suffer so
Yet if you doze on your fluffy throne, then you must doze alone
For did you not think to carve a worthy soul for yourself, a sage for your sanity?
After all, it is a lonely shadow that wiles away his eternity
Shaping a model world for himself, buried deep in childlike thought

And as you mould and paint your spherical canvas
Sculpting mountains with your ancient hands,
Pouring the oceans, careful not to overflow them
As the water cascades through your worn fingers,
Threading your clouds with silver lining, and colouring the sun
With an unwavering brightness from within the melting pot
Do you wonder…
Why, how you came into being?
Ah, but I see the past and the future!
I see a lonely man playing with his marbles, building a world that was once his own
A world reminiscent of former glories
A world drowned in despair without future possibilities
From whence you came
I see you, lone survivor, refugee, orphan—questioning your immortal soul
Locking clay adorned hands as you beg for *our* forgiveness
Tell me my Lord, say the words
Do not be afraid to ask us inferiors—the question that so burdens your brittle mind
Intrigued, I'll ask it myself, if only to spare you the chagrin
If you created man in your own image, then who created you?

Pumpkin Head

Dancing eyes dart nervously as discarded litter runs, skipping alone up the
dusty, desolate streets
The darkness swims heavy as jittery shadows swallow the light
Looking for stained human souls to rip and to eat
Dangling corpse swings hard in the whistling breeze, like Satan's pendulum
Tick tock, tick tock
The time? It's running out fast as Hell's vultures circle the ashen sky as they
begin to flock
Dripping, torn organs drench grotesque pumpkin head, his sadistic grin slashed
Viciously from ear to ear
He bathes euphorically in the red stickiness
Before throwing the world a blood guzzling, sickening leer
Hideous rows of violent teeth, stolen straight out of the jaws of a shark
Rotting flesh dangles, shivering poetically as his bite is most definitely worse
than his bark
Traipsing the broken bones in his suit stitched crudely from human skin

High pitched screams shatter the night air as he plays your spine like the Devil's violin

Plucking the stringy veins furiously with his spindly, skeletal fingers

He plays a blood spattered tune, melancholic, that hauntingly lingers

Looking you up and down as he wiggles his bony digits, like ivory playing spiders alive

The thirst too much as crazed, he seeks more death to exist and to thrive

So on and on he goes, digesting bloodied meal after meal with mindless brutality

The more bodies and souls he devours, the more the myth becomes a reality.

Red Dragon

Red dragon lurks, signifying blood lust
Fiery wrath held in sharp bladed steel
Anger and violence willingly combust
Flames of hatred, malevolence he feels
Victims are but pawns in the game of life
Higher powers seize those who seek the feed
Creeping closer, brandishing Devil's knife
Exposing pure soul, rotting carcass bleeds
Blood hunger satisfied until new moon
Back in the shadows, lapping razor's edge
Quietly smiling, he will be back soon
Deranged mind teetering back from the ledge
Waiting for the next time when he will strive
As the weak shall fall and the strong survive.

Reflection of a Devil's Eye

The shadows on the street loiter, nervous
An obelisk stance… ready to crumble
As that of an oncoming avalanche
Ready to tumble
Hungry to devour the broken weeds
That prop up the fragility of innocence that whispers by, unnoticed
He looks likeable—but I don't like him

I hunt his form within the darkness of common shelter
Staring through smudged glass, and into the night
The steam rises slowly from within the curves of the coffee cup
Cautious, careful
Eyes penetrate the human mist of ghostly swirls
Their trailing presence lost amidst the tired, chattery chaos
"I can feel it."

A twitch of the eye, a delicate quiver of full lip
Questions all within themselves
On the cusp of greatness as softness falls
"Do I, don't I?"
A clever smile adorns my gleaming eye, caught by a shard of jealous light
"Ah, the morality has arisen!"
Dancing left, then right; the power to determine one's fate is a heavy burden
untoward

Clammy hands clenched in a choking silence
Fighting back the increasing dampness as
Metal noise juggernauts at high velocity
The sound of heavy rain blends with the murkiness
Stirring blurred senses
As a voice tells me all is not well within the world
"Yeah, I know," I reply

A transcendence crosses our paths, our souls
He looks up at me, and into my cavernous eyes
Shaken
The mirror cracked indeed.

Rise of the Black Soul

Feverish grin, a mechanical-like arm rises
Eyes bright, fervent as saliva boils on drool excited lips
The anticipation too much—prepare for the chastising
Bloody carnage will ensue, out spring the clawed warships
Arm wound up, ready to strike like a venomous viper
Wild maniacal head shaking, flesh starved screams pierce the cold black night
Taking aim, cheshire cat smile, firing at will like Hell's own private sniper
Grim face, blood spattered, panting heavily in the cold light of day, feeling contrite
If only for a second, a once past life reminiscent
Feeling the soft warm glow of the sun on your blackened heart
A waking shake of fuzzy head, remember who you are, dark adherent
Lightning bolt strike cascading down prominent spine, forces a fiery jump-start
Flaming agony, car crash headache causes onward strides
Slash, hack, rip—death is man's utter despair
In God we trust, yet whom you deride
Go now, job done… leave us to pick up the shattered pieces of life to repair.

Screaming Black Rage

Thunderous eruptions convulse with hate
Electrifying, intensifying
Screaming out black rage as it dominates

As fork lightning barks loud and then dictates
Scorching the earth leaving nature crying
Thunderous eruptions convulse with hate

Striking the night air while the clouds gyrate
Howling winds send old ailing trees flying
Screaming out black rage as it dominates

As the force and power collaborate
Lightning strikes twice and is terrifying
Thunderous eruptions convulse with hate

Rain lashes down cooling all things irate
Distant rumblings are not satisfying
Screaming out black rage as it dominates

The role of master and servant relates
Scared as I am there's no point denying
Thunderous eruptions convulse with hate
Screaming black rage as it dominates.

Seasons

The freshness revives you as you awake
The dewdrops soften the firm bladed grass
As the sun creeps gently over the lake
Early morning birds sing songs as we pass
Into the dawn of a glorious day
Clear blue skies suspend large smokey white clouds
Herald a new season has passed our way
The sunshine beams elegantly and proud
Brown leaves dance quietly in the soft breeze
Like black silhouettes crying silently
Darkness draws closer, you wouldn't believe
Winter's now here, coldness eats violently
Icy harsh nighttimes cause creatures to hide
As the last season flakes out, and has died.

Storm in a World Sized Teacup

Sitting in a crumpled armchair watching a flickering tv, channel surfing
To escape the depressing imagery that burns deep into my retinas
Watching as the world bickers over territories and 'rights' to what they own
Own?! This planet was here long before our species ever was!
Who cuts the pieces of the pie to divide amongst the hungry?
What rights do they have to make such claims? Ah, money talks
There will be no alien invasion, they are up there laughing as they sit back
In their ships watching as we destroy ourselves, saving them the effort
Yes we are unique, a soul that oozes love and empathy
But a tolerance that goes hand in hand with hatred, scorn and violence
What's the point? Governments who tell us what to do, what to eat and when
to shit
But claim they are helping us to be healthy and live longer
Yet refuse us the aid when the living can live no longer!
We shall control your lives, take your money,
But we can't give you what you need because it's all too expensive
Who are they to determine such things?
After all they are only the same as you and I, well I think so
Besides, what makes a healthy, wealthy leader wake up one day
And decide that he wants to shatter the peace of a nation?
Do the lies and greed close their eyes and pin the tail on the map of war?
We don't deserve to prosper as countries build nuclear and chemical weapons
Desperate to use on anyone that crosses that drawn line in the Earth's sand
What makes us so special that we can stuff our faces full of food

Yet watch children who ask for nothing, die of hunger and thirst?
We consume the designer brands, yes a nice jumper
The cost of which would feed a poor African family for six months
But let's turn that sad tv commercial over, "that's how they get you," we say
The genuine good are the few
The few that quietly make a slight scratch of decency on the surface of the glass
As we look in
Deep down, we are all guilty of committing crimes against humanity
Whether it's a war, or throwing away a tasteless meal
Yet climate change is probably a natural cycles that occurs every 100,000 years
But instead of keeping it at its current rate we decide to quicken it
Yes, let's not worry about it now, leave it to the next generation to deal with
They will know what to do, shhh! They can front the cost if we keep quiet
They might even devise a proper justice system whilst they are at it
A system that actually punishes the bad, giving them food for thought
Anything would be better than nothing, though nothing
Is all that is ever promised as hollow words fall from hollow mouths
War, hatred, violence, lies, fear, greed, broken lives and death
Sometimes I think it would be poetic justice to watch the world intricately crumble.

Tears of an Angel

The reflective, watery globe slides gracefully south
Zig-zagging the smooth terrain towards her quivering, open mouth
Tear-laden eyes glance upwards as her halo heavy head bows down
Drenching all beneath who can't swim, crying uncontrollably
Helpless as they drown
The pain etched on her pure pale canvas, truly heartbreaking
The constant pull on her innocent soul causes His bitter, venomous snaking
Delicate hands, like vines, entwined in desperate prayers as crux of the matter
Harp strings snap as her cries cause a thousand halos to shatter
Into an ash swamped snow, floating feather-like from wings unfurled
Disintegrating into charcoal dust as it enters the rotten core of humanity's world.

The 24 Hour Life of a Party Seeking Crane Fly

Born into the world on a damp autumn morning
Amongst the dew infested green blades as the sun is dawning
A gentle breeze casts the smell of the earth far and wide
The fly devours its first dusky breath deep down inside

The air tickles its transparent wings as it gingerly stretches them out
Taking in the new found surroundings, chortling through its pencil-like snout
Where's the party at?
From one generation to the next, born and bred
Only 24 hours to learn to fly, party, and get laid before its dead

Dazzled by the bright lights, striking colour and worldly sounds
Legs flailing, it dances erratically like a hypnotised clown
Vibrating through the calm, surfing the invisible wave
Cautious, yet excited as it climbs ever higher, looking to misbehave

Its minuscule eyes, sensitive on tubular storks
Ears suddenly pricked at the karaoke voices singing "New York, New York"
A tiny delighted flutter as it heads down towards the raucous shindig
Jiggling limbs as it warms up for its one and only disco gig

Slowing up in the darkness, something isn't right
Struggling to breath, its wasted time flying all night!
The sounds of the party fade in echoic whispers
The rhythm floating further away as the chill becomes crisper

It lies mournfully in the fields, staring at the weak glow of the fresh morning light
24 hours have come full circle, and there's no partner or another party in sight.

The Better Man

Blood boiling, flowing through pumped veins like lava from a raging volcano
Curling lips reveal violent, gritted teeth as venomous tongue coils like an angry snake
Trapped in a pearl cage
Searing pain slices the brain as thumping heart threatens to explode at the point of no return
Chest swelling as deep breaths are consumed, calmly attempting to dowse the fire within
Split down the middle as the balance comes into play, agonising decision
Which way will it sway?
Clenched fists turn skin pale, headstrong like a disturbed bull, ready for the fight
Stop and think… one minute of madness can turn into a lifetime of sadness and regret
Be cool, think of a serene ocean, count to ten, be the better man
Walk away
Let them laugh, for they do not see their wasted future that lies ahead
They mock as they think they have won, but the real winner celebrates quietly as he lives
To fight another day.

The Change

The biting breeze sinks its jagged fangs into drought-riddled skin
Head bowed against the attack, eyes squint as coldness causes stinging wet
To trickle like a weaving snail, leaving its silvery trail over rough lines
Heavy snowflakes float gracefully, rocking back and forth like ships lost at sea
Redness in numb cheeks travels outwards like ripples from a disturbed pond
Angry at being awoken by a stone's throw
Orange glow from steel soldiers paves the path with good intentions
Danger lurks on all corners as shrivelled heart works hard
Adrenaline teetering on the edge
Paranoid footsteps crunch behind hunched shell, quicker and louder
As sweat induced fear expels itself cautiously

Dampness sits tight, waiting for its moment of glory
When it will proudly spill into racing, watery crystals
Blue veins stand to attention underneath woollen barracks
As blood orders the flow
Tick, tick, tick, fragile mind counts down to instinctive, animalistic explosion
Large flaming black wings, attached to the bizarre
Erupt as piercing howls emanate from red eyes that burn painfully
Frozen shaking hands, raised in defence, aim to protect
As crumpled face turns away from ear bleeding screams
Defeated, knees sore as they hit black ice, freezing
The wetness clawing its way up stiff denim as it soaks in relentlessly
Quivering hands clasped desperately as gibbering prayers sputter out
A flow of cold, steam-like blasts from chattering white pearls
Eyes open... nothing,
Take heed, you have been warned
The future has already been written.

The Death of England's Rose

Beating heart fades like a wilting flower, dying slowly
As its brittle petals weep into the wind on a harsh winter's day,
The dried up fragments disappear into the air, forever lost like a broken soul
Staring back at the devastation that is left behind
The pain too much to bear as the fractured stem reaches out desperately
Yearning for the petals' return to make it whole again
The only parting gift is eternal loneliness
Echoes of sorrow shattering the fragile mind of its existence
The withered stem recoils in a sadness that suffocates it into submission
Its cries vibrating through the dry dusty earth as all of nature listens quietly…
Torn from the roots of birthplace and grave
Nonchalantly tossed on the compost scrapheap of life, only to be cruelly re-
cycled again
The red colourful glory reduced to a depressing brown tinge,
Like dead empty eyes that have lost their once proud sparkle
Heavy cement sky wrings out its tears that fall purposely;
A last watery drink to toast a bonfire cremation
Silhouettes of angry flames sway dominantly in the cold breeze, shoulder to
shoulder
As they look down their hot noses in defiance at the flowery congregation
The twirling, dancing black smoke fights its way up into the thick air
Grinning sadistically at what the future holds
The surrounding peaceful beauty bow their heads, in respect at the death of
England's rose.

The Dogged Angel

Disengaged from society, why? Man's best friend
She won't lie, hate, reject or betray me, only love me to the bitter end
As I recoil from the splintered spine of human nature's dark
In my blackest hour, the light shines through her echo-laden bark
The diehard loyalty, the effervescent energy, it all knows no bounds
When my spirit breaks, she turns and hunts me down like a bloodhound
The tenacious terrier qualities burn bright as she seeks to console me
Her wagging tail speaks volumes, it says: "cheer up, it is time for my tea!"
In a time when a fractured, frenetic Britain screams loud
She doesn't even know what she does, but her love and affection lift the darkest
of clouds.

The Evils of Our Dead

Dead souls ignite to rain fire and brimstone
Screaming black death in revenge at life
The horrors we witness scrape deep the bone

Killers become immortalised in stone
Making innocent people suffer strife
Dead souls ignite to rain fire and brimstone

Not selling their souls just merely for loan
Ready to carve up the world with a knife
The horrors we witness scrape deep the bone

Wishing they were gods in worlds of their own
Rumours of war in our domains are rife
Dead souls ignite to rain fire and brimstone

Hell's soldiers ready to fight for the throne
Killing and maiming and taking your wife
The horrors we witness scrape deep the bone

Each one destroyed evil seeds are now sown
No more do the marchers play with their fifes
Dead souls ignite to rain fire and brimstone
The horrors we witness scrape deep the bone.

The Fallen Angel

Questioning eyes drink in the slow drizzle of black ash
That falls endlessly from the heavens
Hands held out at the sides as he waits to be drenched in a downpour of wrath
A stunned silence… hypnotic, as the awe-filled beauty floats
Like majestic crows feathers
Teardrops sparkle, akin to a millionaire's diamonds
That cut pricelessly into the glass skin
Glorious flowers of exquisite colour, shrivelled to brown crisps
The angels howl in despair
A darkened world, stained by the blood of the innocent
That pools into a flaming lava of anguish; the rage bubbling under the surface
Angels tears shower the world in a violent hailstorm
Battering the soil in jealousy at their Lord's never ending mortal forgiveness
The last man alive, why can't anyone love him?
He now knows what it is to feel human as his halo melts
Like milk running through soft hands
Destined to walk blindly—forsaken—lost on God's highway

The wanderer who hitches on past memories as this is all he possesses
Cursed for being himself, an imperfect machine in an imperfect world
A deep rooted desolation, that branches out like sticky tentacles, choking the life
The balance between the Earth's pure and impure
Strikes a delicate, yet lonely chord
As all around crumbles, falling eloquently away
The sour taste of life, like poisonous wine from a rusted goblet
Flows like a corrupt sea through his charred veins
He pleads to the angels for guidance, but prayers fall on deaf ears
As the changing tides beg to cleanse the soul of the earth
The fallen angel cries alone.

The Fearful Soul

Heaven smiles as golden rays pierce the suspended clouds,
Arrowing down like trails of light from giant torches
Swamping weary old features with a glowing warmth

Birds harsh singing stabs unapologetically
As it whistles into sensitive ears, puncturing the senses
Tired soul cringes sharply as a blast of soft light hits glazed eyes
Terrifying the worn face before it cautiously recoils
Back away into the safety of the shadows

Heavy heart, shrivelled like a piece of dried rotten fruit
Struggles to contain energy as the blood is too afraid to enter the valleys of life
Aching head, taunted by life movies of a long ago past
Threatens to explode as the screeching songs skewer the throbbing brain

Shaking leathery-skinned hands fail miserably
As they attempt to cover wrinkled ears from the oncoming bite
Contorted face signifies the painful flashes of a photographic memory
The images burn deep into the psyche
As it spins uncontrollably

Devil's grin basks in the warm glow like a sunbathing sin
Teary eyes fight to focus on the white feather
That falls majestically to the dry green grass
The saltiness stinging, disorientating the clarity as sanity is questioned

Noises from ordinary lives surround the soul, engulfing it in slow motion
Forcing it to close itself off from a split world in pain
Broken body collapses into a ball, desperate to evade the trials of life
To forget that it even exists, but to no avail

A pitiful look to the bright blue, a look that befits begging—pleading to be taken
Dragged from the horrors of a corrupt and damaged planet
Waiting for answers that never come.

The Forgotten

A harsh breeze ruffles the bladed fields like God's angry breath
Sighing heavily in forlorn disappointment
Birds twitter in unison, crying sadly at his disapproval
Before flying delicately away
The falling rain, soaked up by the earth that acts as nature's tissue
Dabbing the tears of Heaven
A high pitched chorus of distraught screams fall from the mouths of the reborn
Shattering the halos of a thousand angels
The millions of pieces float melancholically in the air
Like pure crisp snowflakes on a quiet winter's day
The brokenhearted look to the ceiling of the earth
Pleading for an intervention as they lucidly push aside the protective cloud cushions
In their desperate search for something more beyond
Souls stir restlessly around the living, swirling contemptuously
As they attempt to influence the confused good with whispers
That fall on deaf ears
Weathered hands clasped tight in prayer, empty words disappear
Into empty space as they turn their back on the world
The devastation colossal, as one's faith shuns oneself

The abandonment too much to bear as a stuttering heart drops more beats
Down the vacant well
Aching crunch as tired knees hit hard ground before curling up
Childlike in a ball, rocking back and forth in aggrieved silence
Thunderous applause erupts in Earth's amphitheatre
The audience?
Fractured spirits of wasted lives, lost to a violent past
Who's left to pick up the pieces of a trembling, shredded life,
To use humanity to glue the soul back together?
Aggressive hands pound the lonely head
Only oneself can truly find the answers deep within the gaping black void
Is it all a test of faith? A faith in oneself and a faith in the unknown
That lays the weary path ahead
If life is the test, then we have failed it miserably.

The Gates of Wrath

Through the rusted gates of wrath we fall
Hand in hand, deep into the watery chasm of bile
Down, until toes achingly brush the sands, we stand tall
Cussing the merriment, seeking to defile

A delicate whisper of breeze
Flatters the curtain as that to enmesh
With flittering interruptions back and forth to deceive
Scratch pen on paper, not blade on flesh

Is the invidious, yet cursory memory of past life pains
So we strive to craft one another from paper;
To soak up—to blot—our sins, our pernicious stains
That hang over our skeletons like wet washing, drowning the dry draper

Life fills the lungs, though not with a vitality
But the watery burden appeases the conscience
Oh, how I see! Oh, now I see!
That you build your hay wall, only for me to burn it down
With pugnacious sentiment, and a pestilent dominance

But please forgive me
For now I see! Oh, how I see!

The Great Escape

Dry, dead leaves scuttle sideways up the empty street
Like crabs, lost on a desolate beach as they search for their watery home
Old branches lash out furiously, their arms controlled by invisible strings
From the windy puppet master

Harsh rain pelts the soul, the fierce drops sting my weathered skin
As pin pricks from a violent sewing machine
The demonic wind howls like a banshee, the screams perforate the eardrums
That cause distorted features

A familiar face, lost in the past, grimaces in embarrassment as she ghosts past
me
Squinted eyes strive to focus as my neck cranes a backwards glance
The elements continue to distract me
The sadness, etched painfully on my facial canvas is designed for her eyes only

Thick droplets of rain fall heavy, bouncing clumsily before rolling steeply away
I see the shadows on the water moving purposely yet calm
The storm will inevitably follow

Plastic bags snap violently in the aggressive breeze
As their owners bury their razor whipped faces into the concrete sand
Death as dark as the sky swirls from soul to soul
Sniffing who is ripe amongst the oblivious

My skin agitates as though there's something nasty underneath it
Desperately trying to claw its way out
My empty shell drifts aimlessly, alive yet dead beneath the surface
The lights are on but I'm simply not home

A grin of piano keys awaken me as they ramble on and on
Out of tune as they ask how I am
A flicker of false interest masks my distaste at such meaningless encounters
I seek escape from the monotony of such pleasantries

The over active mouth spews silent words as I nod in agreement
I take the blame, sorry for wasting their time in a polite effort to walk away
Relief flows like warm waves crashing softly over my delicate fragility
I wander on blindly

Another smile begins to reel me in from the crowd
I sigh tiredly as the cycle starts over again
Images of another day, a world away spread lukewarm around my head
Like spilt oil growing outwards, drowning me in a syrupy thickness

I stand unable to move, the oil greases the life that starts my engine moving
Steve McQueen jumps over my brain on his motorbike, crashing through my life
The Great Escape, that's all that matters
Escape.

The Halo Army

End of the world beckons as angels on horseback thunder into the depths of
Hell
Gleaming immortal swords raised aloft during Heaven's war cry
The heat singes wings, reducing fraying white feathers to a burning smell
The charcoal enemy scuttle into battle below the red and black flaming sky

Gigantic catapults release fireballs that streak amber through the darkest parts,
aimed at the pure
Spitting embers strike like bullets, cauterising, clipping the wings of oncoming
avengers
Flailing hooves beat at invisible enemies
Get up, rise, fight and endure

Dancing on hot coals, creeping closer, here come the needle-toothed scavengers
Procure the ash castle, release innocent souls, send them forth across the divide
Into God's warm embrace
Point the Lord's steel forwards, rally the halo army, prepare for bloody carnage
Charge!

Howling souls reach for the blinding light, it's close now as warmth and eu-
phoria interlace
Take the downward spiral as demonic soldiers scatter to the land of the living,
at large
Send out the archangel Gabriel, the sheriff between these translucent parts
Crack the Lord's whip, round up the fire breathing cattle branded 666

Protect God's children, blanket them with love from an angel's voice
As for now peace will reign in the Kingdom of Heaven
Until the beast himself conjures up dark new tricks.

The Jaws of War

Deep breaths as the knotted web of grief entwines itself around a broken heart
Like fishing line wrapped around a defenceless, dying animal
Coiling, tightening as the life force bleeds out
Before the darkness begins to smother the fading light

Cold, empty eyes stare out from beneath the war painted false mask
The etched lines portraying its tough, lived in qualities
Shivering soul screams for warmth as it hides
Beneath the harsh, empty shell of humanity

Transparent fists pound on bone walls of the human prison cell
Begging to be released from a world of unknown hatred
Sun's warm glare rebounds off dead glassy eyes, the shine glimmering
As reflective mirrors, as droplets of salty water drown out any remaining life

A thumping heart the only sound that echoes
Through the quiet panic as the tension on strings pulls rigid
Deafening booms explodes the eardrums, sending all into a muted daze as
Grimy bodies soaked in lukewarm sweat, stagger

They attempt to gain their bearings in the fiery, bloody rain
Hot grit and sand torture the eyes
Turning them into repetitive blinking camera shutters
That capture an album of unwanted pictures

Thick black smoke attacks the lungs
Choking them violently as all around struggle for survival
Blood smeared trembling hands desperately try to drag fallen heroes to safety
The pain shared as a glance at faces in agony reveals all

The muscle destroying effort joins hands with the crumbling mental structure
Before skipping off together down nightmare avenue
These are the jaws of war my friends, ready to swallow you whole
It is time you came home.

The Leap

Tired eyes clenched shut, look to the heavens as strong winds threaten to push,
like invisible hands
Ravaged soul, encased in fragile shell, teeters back and forth in robotic dance
On life's slippery ledge
Crushed spirit can take no more as God weeps for his children
His tears drowning the city all around
Dry mouth, silent cries, and sore throat as stabbing screams echo inside
Of jumbled head as shaking fingers bore through throbbing temples
What will go first, the heart or the body?
Tiny life goes on as the bet is made
Saying goodbye with quiet whispers, time to forgive oneself
Arms open, welcoming as the moment of truth arrives in tip toeing, childlike
forward steps
Relax, visualise a beautiful, crystal clear swishing ocean
Here comes the leap…
All of Heaven howls as harp-strings snap
Sad angels bury sobbing heads into feathery hands
The cold whistling breeze, the only sound as it shaves the face like a razor's edge
Windows pass one after the other as time stands still
Like a sideways train passing fast

Childhood memories glow like warm sunshine in fields of gold
Don't worry, the end is coming as serene smile welcomes eternal peace
Darkness, silence, nothingness
Running, shuffling feet crowd round as broken soul lay paralysed
Suffocating in a crawling pool of blood
Eyes bouncing in all directions, watching the living, as disgusted mouths spew silent screams
White feather falls tantalisingly to the floor, bobbing up and down as it floats
Stranded in an unfamiliar sea of red
Wanting to reach out and save it
But can't move as it succumbs to the overwhelming life force that declines rapidly
One last glance as refreshed eyes look down upon the shattered shell and it's fading light
The shine dissipating forever.

The Lonely Boy

The lonely boy chases the shadows
Riding the coattails of the flighty breeze
Tearing through his silky dark hair
As it guides his broken hearted innocence into the forest
Past the solid green and brown giants
That sway in teasing whispers
As he seeks the soul of happiness lost,
He reaches out as she ghosts by silently
Clutching at past memories, her essence spirited away
Scattering on the wind as ash confetti
Long dead as vibrant energies confuse his glassy, marble-like empty eyes
The Lords of the forest cry to Mother Nature
Begging for his forgiveness as he yearns to be loved
To be wanted with affection, not pity
The soft rain tiptoes around all, attempting a sorrowful diversion
Pitter-pattering on the firm leaves in a rhythmic, watery tango
As the chance of real love evaporates into the hazy mist
Vanishing like a lighthouse beacon that fades into a dark blanket
From salt worthy eyes that bob helplessly upon choppy seas,
The boat crashes into the heavy heart, sinking
As the lonely boy grieves for himself.

The Loner

Who am I? I don't know
Through the winding paths of my mind, gone is the life glow
A place in the world for me, yet to be earned
Every twisted dead end leaves my frail bridges burned
Lost in a swirling maze of blurriness, like a scared rat scampering for freedom
Fear of drowning in an unpredictable society, who will lead them?
I watch forlornly as puree dribbles like food lava from a baby's volcanic mouth
Sliding disgustingly slow in a giant heap as it heads due south
Those frantic cries echo those of the insane, lost inside a grey prison
The keys are themselves
Unlocking the knowledge shall give us all the wealth
Yet elderly people struggle in their second life battle for survival, gingerly fighting to stay proud
As I weep inside, knowing that one day it will be me disappearing into the crowd.

The Lost

Lonely soul stands stranded, lost in a sea of stars as it desperately searches
The black void for answers
Reaching vision scours the heavens, storing images of the cosmos
Into the album of the mind, ready to remember them at a moments notice
A weepy trail runs like a salty river, as it navigates its way down and over
A lived-in terrain, staring hypnotically at the beauty of the twinkling darkness
Juddered rudely awake as the whistling pierces the eardrums
Like pencil holes jabbed through paper, the war has begun
Commands left, commands right, shaking hand holds sweat-laced, itchy helmet
Eyes strain to focus through the smothering smoke

Attempting to follow the shadows in front of them, and to safety
In the arena of chaos
Pop, pop, pop, the sky lights up in booming flashes of white before dimming out
Leaving a thick smoky haze that swims lazily through the violent air
Quiet, the shell casing rain eases after drenching all around in a metal wetness
A look cast upwards, a few seconds to ponder whether anyone up there
Is looking down upon this world
And if they are, then what must they think?
Sadness? Disgust? Terror? Who knows, but one question is clear:
Are we a race worth saving?
Each and every man, woman and child can only decide for themselves
As they choose their own paths in life
Trembling bodies, some no more than children themselves, pray for home
Taking comfort in future memories yet to be written, should they survive
Survive? Only to be drawn from one conflict and sent straight into another
Now that is truly the sad part.

The Love I Can Never Have

Your mellifluous tones swim alluringly around my head in velvety throngs
An intoxicating caress on my senses, that result in my joie de vivre abandon-
ment
In a brief, yet salacious moment
The glimpse of your milky thigh leaves me begging, wishing and praying
As I graze your pale-skinned beauty, aroused by your arousal
My trembling fingers dance seductively higher, sliding like a new born foal
on ice
As I gaze into your magnetic blue eyes
That swim in front of your mighty intelligence as
You stare back at me, your smile dazzling my excited eyes
Eyes that have been dead for an age,
And your smile… My God, your smile!
Your smile that yanks my heartstrings,
Playing them in divine whispers that I succumb to effortlessly
Making my heart dance to your exquisite tune
You are the puppeteer to my raging, ravenous soul
I would die for you
The goosebumps heightened, only serve to jolt—electrify—my every fibre
Into life
Like lightening striking my skin, raising, singeing every hair on my body to ash
In a monolithic moan of ecstatic anticipation
Waiting
As my hands snake—slither up towards your full breasts

Gently teasing, cupping and carefully caressing the smooth,
Delectable contours of their firmness
That satisfies my every whim and desire
I press my full lips against the ageless beauty of your supple neck
Kiss after kiss
Your sumptuous slenderness bends, and your head slowly tilts backwards
Your generous wavy hair bounces and brushes against my fever
Sweeping, like a tidal wave of comfort that says "you are mine forever,"
As I close my eyes, drinking in your essence
My dream can never be
You I love are loved, and in love with another
My heartbreaking loneliness is too much of a burden to carry
For my grieving soul
Yet this happiness and dream I must sacrifice
For I am morally bound by my soul, as God is my witness
To forego my happiness, to save and prevent the destruction of others
As much as it drowns my heart in a choking whirlpool of emotion
I must let go
But the worst part?
You will never know how I feel.

The Only Way is Essex

The wooden bench offers deserved consolation as I rest my tired soul
Gazing out far and wide at the cool blue from the grassy cliff top verge
The swishing calm glistens like diamonds
As the sun's yellow glow penetrates the watery riches
A nice breeze ruffles my sweaty hair as I shield my eyes
From the ever increasing brightness
A few seconds, that's all it takes, as I forget where I am
As the beauty hypnotises the sadness into submission
In these glorious moments, I am the only man alive
I feel the dead weight of the darkness lifted, dragged and drowned at sea
Windsurfers scatter the watery void, their sails pointing like arrow tips
As they engage in a charging glide towards the foamy shore
Screaming seagulls chase fallen chips and ice cream
That lay wounded with a child's awkward footprint still embedded in it
Angry insects buzz aggressively as they seek their fill of the days sugary treats
Children whoop with delight at the fun they're having
Playing furiously as though tomorrow is the end of the world
The sun worshippers dot the golden sand expertly
Each oblivious to those around them as they quietly crave their fix
The warm glow comforts my face, revitalising the body
Like a rechargeable battery, breathing new life into old parts
I stare, mesmerised as the scenes all come together like a picturesque postcard
The image painted on to a canvas in my mind
They say the only way is Essex, I think they may just be right.

The Red Field

We sit shoulder to shoulder, side by side
Joking, laughing, my brothers and I
As we make the best of the wet earth and it bleak surroundings,
The raindrops descend heavily, trampolining clumsily off our thin plastic pon-
chos
Extending to our weapons that offer a cold love standing between our knees
Our aching backs rest harsh against the moist walls of soil

The thunderous echoes constantly shake our conversations of home
Especially the tales I regale of family life
As I seek to divert frightened eyes that peer upwards into the night
Now turned into day
In brilliant white flashes of foreign languages and smoky, parachuted silhou-
ettes

My shoulders grow tense as we each feel the domino effect of silent fear
Every youthful face shows a bravery through gritted teeth
Clenched in a mask of teenage manhood
Scared of what the others may think if the truth is known

Voices crawl closer as my Captain barks the orders
We think of home, we think of home
I slide the crumpled snapshot of my beautiful wife into my top pocket
Patting it down safely—ritualistically—with trembling hands
Smiling as the memorised images of her dancing seductively play in my head
My God, your dancing, I love your dancing. I love you...

Thousands of white knuckles glow
As grip tighten around the triggers of their steel comfort blankets
Hugging the hardness, protective and alone come their darkest hour
Some recite broken fragments of poetry
Me? I take solace in the Bible, the 23rd psalm:
Though as I walk through the valley of the shadow of death—

The whistle blows, its shrillness turning us all into vomiting wrecks
My brothers and I charge out from our dank, mud-strewn trenches
Into the raucous black of Hell
Running tiredly on clay hampered legs
Wet socks squelching in mouldy leather boots
Shouting obscenities we *never* dare say out loud back home
Crying
My heart sinks as I leave a sodden footprint upon my fallen brother's chest

Drizzled bayonets glimmer within the jerking flow of burning flares
Like shards of glass arrows that bear down upon my enemy
I can't wait to go home and kiss my wife, to hold her close
But blood curdling screams seep into the murky corners of my dreams
Until the wounded pray no more

Only the birds sing sweetly as the bold sun wakes up
Casting aside the twilight nightmares
Shining a light across the dew-laden, bloody red field.

The Running Boy

The hazy sunshine glows, offering a comforting warmth
As it casts its soft breath over the harsh green fields
The excitable boy climbs the splintered old wooden gate
Before running headstrong through the blankets of hovering insects
That glide obliviously under the yellow calmness

Jumping and skipping

Dodging the golden trumpets that stand proud
As they release their song to the clear blue sea in the sky
Spinning and weaving
Zig-zagging through the waist high corn grenades
That wait to explode come the day

He races all as he seeks his ecstatic finishing line
Grubby white canvas trainers bounce off the dry solid earth
As he waves the stick in his hand like a magic wand
Summoning more carefree happiness

A silky breeze ruffles his already messy dark hair as he flies
The arms of his orange windbreaker jacket, knotted tight around his neck
Flapping, snapping outwards like a boat's sail as he navigates the grassy oceans
Into the thick ancient trees that dance rhythmically to his youthful tune

Birds twitter cautiously overhead
Unsure of the high pitched laughter that echoes their own voices
Ready to take flight at a moments notice as
Angry ants gesture as their homes are innocently crushed underfoot

As the bundle of effervescent energy knows no bounds
No stopping until he reaches home.

The Trials of England's Rose

Dew slides heavily from the solid red rose, like watery guilt,
Drenching the thirsty earth with its shameful sins
The desolate, dusty ground drinks greedily
As it seeks to purify the burdened flower
Its stem carrying the weight of nature upon its fragile green shoulders
Its once bright royal red, a beacon of shining light and hope
That stood proudly above the darkness, guiding the souls of the lost safely home
Britannia rules the waves? The days of the Great are gone forever, vanquished
In a swirling black sea of fear and depression, drowning the innocent
The goodness and morality that once meant something to us all,
Crushed underneath the feet of the young, violent hyenas that prowl the lands

The crisp petals fall one by one, like overwhelmed cities
Swamped by the unjust that have no desire to feel
The glorious colour drained completely dry, like an old piece of discarded clothing
Forced through a mangler, choking violently
As the last drops of crystal clear life escape from the corrupt dark of night
The roses that bloomed from the past, allowed us the freedoms we so desperately craved
Now turn in their forgotten flowerbed graves
Weeping at the betrayal on parade before them
The empty shells of a damaged generation, too much
As the stem's spine snaps under the wave of the do-gooders
Splintering as ferociously as its own psyche

The shrinking violets turn the other cheek, purposely oblivious to the coming end
As the decrepit rose lay broken, all around silently mourn
Burying their heads as the heavens part, bringing forth the tears of a millennia
Dead eyes refuse to focus on a budding new life,
But the young rose is ready to bloom from the ashes of a crippled nation
Begging to be reborn, like a superhero with its red petalled cape
Standing defiantly against the ills of society
Ready to rise and endure the so-called path paved with good intentions.

The Two Faces of Man

Blood red sun curdles, ravenous corpse craves
Black wings in mist, reprehensible frown
Hunting misanthropists, desolate braves
Leviathan beast wears scurrilous crown
Churning metamorphosis, men of rage
Deranged individuals lachrymose
Delighted at life in fiery cage
Hazy, thunderous screams are comatose
Chainsaw Charlie shredding withered old flesh
Sacrificial bones sense cupidity
Cantankerous nightmare, awake now fresh
Invisible force breeds vitality
Screaming black hearts in violent convulsion
Marionette dancing in repulsion

The Watcher

Watery crystals fall mesmerisingly from the concrete sky
As bloodshot eyes tell their own story
Rough, fleshy hand lies flat on cool glass, occasionally steamed up
By a grief stained warm breath
Weary forehead feeling left out, presses against the glass
Joining the hand in unison as it seeks a calming influence
Cracks adorn a once smooth face as the weathered brow loses its footing
Sloping towards the bridge, like melting ice
Millions of hairs stand upright as sergeant brain orders its troops
Ready for active duty
A shiver descends over the zombie-like trance, stroking the fine hairs
Like a summer's breeze caressing lush green fields
Pearl tombstones grind menacingly tight
As the memory frames old photographs taken by the soul
Lifeless fingers slide slowly down the misty glass
Playing a sad tune as they leave their trail marks behind, lost
Split heart crumbles with each pulsing beat
The pieces disappearing into a chasm as deep as its own sensitivity
Eyelids close gently as painful memories replay themselves over and over

Like a scratched, broken record
The stylus jabs hard, a never forgiving pin pricking that fries the nervous system
Into a numb depression
Long, drawn out sigh signals everlasting loneliness
Hopeful net catches the heart's falling debris
Only to become an entwined, suffocating tangled mess like a trapped fish out of water
Cold spasming hands grasp at the chest as breathlessness takes charge
Shutters come down over dead eyes, the lips curl as the mask slips
Shut up shop, its time to go home.

Through the Windows of a Lonely Soul

The trees sway hypnotically in the strong breeze, rhythmically
As though performing some ritualistic, ancient dance
Large clouds blanket them from behind, offering protection wrapped in cotton wool as
The bleakness moves closer
Crunching leaves from nature's sounds take me away a hundred millennia
To a time when things were simpler, quieter
The golden globe strives to escape from its dark clouded prison
Pushing forcefully as it tries to shed some warm light on its subjects
The large pond ripples wide, warning me not to disturb it, to leave it alone
Before settling peacefully, allowing me to stay if I'm quiet
Flowery aromas—sweet—assault the senses pleasantly
Scaling the heights of my nasal canal, reaching the top in an explosion of scented lava
An empty crisp packet races by teasingly, begging me to chase after it before taking flight
Leaves me trailing behind
I should expect no less, this is the story through the windows of a lonely soul.

Underworld

Poisonous tongue, sour, grim taste, bitter soul
Barbed wire embrace coiling, slicing cold, spirit failing
Skating on blood, psychotic, like newborn foal
Organs ground as fleshy tune plays, monkey wailing
Eyes alive, hatred burns acidic vengeance
Remnant of bloody glories past… a toast! Goblet upside down
Severed memories, fractured psyche forms violent allegiance
Ravenous legions bite cruel,
Ah the flow, as tears from an empty clown
Tap, tap, tap, red pool simmers in flaming earth
Time is a healer? No, a decrepit cancer!
Salvation teases, buzzing like flies around a corpse, now prove your worth!
Flame licked silhouette, vile necromancer
Crushing pangs of emptiness twist hard
Spidery hands rip harsh to expose the forgotten, not so kindly
Game over, insert another sin—lost on a high card!
Alone in the world, the bitter soul wanders blindly.

Urban Renewal

Polemic, smash that fool, rip his gold teeth
Cut the Gordian knot, send him a wreath
No conscience, I'm no collaborator
I'm the one and only dominator
Found my spiracle— I can breathe, relief!
Rise to the top, I've earned the belief
To hunt and kill like an alligator
Too late for the passive mediator
You know when you die you're going beneath
I, kleptomaniac do so bequeath
The immutable face of self-rupture
Cursed your soul, original corruptor
Protecting your vicious soul underneath
If only for a while, keeping it brief
Polemic, smash that fool, rip his gold teeth
Cut the Gordian knot, send him a wreath.

Urban Renewal 2

Ascending from the crumbling white slums
Your vocation in life? A drug addicted street bum
Crawling round acting greedy and mean
All you're after is your precious green
Breaking bones, you draconian motherfucker
Crushing, burning your rivals, cocksucker
Taking over, the cream rises to the top
You've earned your chance—grab it before you drop
Smoking out the fake plastic gangsters
No one left to laugh at the original prankster
I'm the king of kings as I sit on my throne
Hand in hand with my mobile phone
Day to day I destroy urban rubble
No motherfucker's gonna burst my bubble
Kill or be killed, that's my motto
Devil's hunting me from his big black grotto
Face to face around the wishing well
One left standing, one in Hell.

Watching the World Burn

The droplets of rain crash down hard against the windows
Like shards of glass glistening in the moonlight
Plop, plop, plop, echoes the watery few, lost in a tiny river
That gently ripples in the broken dish that lives on the porch outside

Sad eyes peer out into the darkness, looking for something—anything
Through the nervous condensation that clings lovingly to its glass lover
The quiet soothes until natures hidden nightlife comes alive, it's their time now
The porch light flickers as insects fly to their death
Hypnotised by the light and its false promises... the electrifying buzz ends them
A guilty sigh does little to appease

Distant rumbles suggest that all is not happy with the world
Batten down the hatches, a storm is coming
Creatures of the night struck silent, alert as quivering noses sniff the oppressive sky
Before scattering to safety

The thick warm air turns cool as the trees rustle, dancing elegantly
From side to side as the branches hold hands as in ritual
Dead insects crackle on the wooden floor before being blown recklessly off
And into the long grassy, dusty graveyard

The simplicity of it all, evident as the old black and white TV hisses and whines
Static interference as yet more war, hatred and death dominate every channel
The warriors of yesterday cry into the earth as
The freedoms—fought for us so bravely during every war—almost lost
As the hand of censorship clamps tight over the mouths of those who speak out

Sheets of light far away flash on and off
The strong breeze directs the wet crystals on to the porch decking
Forcing backward shuffles

Broken beer bottles congregate in the corner of the dry yard
Like a glass gang, jagged and fierce, ready for blood
The wind whistles over their tops
Playing a melancholic tune that keeps them at bay, mesmerised

Dark clouds slide ever closer as the Devil flits in and out of the shadows
Though things would be happier if the rose tinted glasses could be found
A weary, depressing sigh signals enough is enough
As the booze drenched souls argue long into the night

I rock back and forth on the porch in my decadent wooden chair
Gazing forlornly at the jittery sky
Sometimes I think it would be better to just watch the world burn.

Welcome to the War

Delicate, skeletal fingers gently trace the contours of the cold face
Snaking their way deceivingly as harsh eyes lock horns
Black, empty soul stares intimidatingly as a banshee's scream pierces the falsely lulled senses
Into painful submission
Dagger-like nails dig violently into unprotected skull
Pulling frightened face ever nearer the vacuous, open mouth
Aching head vomits silent screams as the warm trickles negotiate the difficult terrain
Before dropping from the face of the living earth
Rattled brain causes psychotic twitches as eyes clench hard against the effort
A tooth and nail fight between the opposite worlds ensues, call out the halo army!
Rumbling chaos all around as nervous eyes shriek open sharply
GET UP! GET UP!

Rough hands grip the quivering face tight, shaking it hard as eyes strive
To focus like an aggressive camera lens
The reality comes crashing down all around as clarity reigns supreme
Bullets whistle by, screeching like venomous beasts from Hell,
Howling in excitement at the conflict before them
Loose body floats up from the dusty ground as explosions ring round,
Dry heaving as heavy head—filled with movies of home—falls back
Sergeant's vocal cage booms into disoriented face, like a shockwave from a
sonic blast
Saliva shrapnel grazing the flesh
Searing pain stabs the eardrums as sweat, blood and tears, that hold their own
nightmares,
Are scattered in all directions
Soldiers dance like crazed marionettes as they attempt to cut loose from their
strings
And seek cover from the Hell zone
Dirty sweat stings gritted, lifeless eyes as thick plumes of smoke begin to choke
charcoal lungs
Into waving the white flag
Some say: "today is a good day to die."
How wrong they are, how wrong they are.

Who the Fuck is Cedric?

The sun's glare blinds me, briefly forcing me to see dazzling white spots
Dancing before my eyes
An ear popping, screeching sound terrifies me as I raise my grubby,
Quivering hands to block out the light
A harsh voice screams out, deafening me, disorientating me as I cringe
Open mouthed from the verbal bomb
"Get down!" I think the phlegm croaked voice shouts, but I'm not sure
I can't hear properly
Two large hands thump into my back, causing me to fall flat on my face
As the dirt and sand sticks to my sweat covered face, tickling my eyelashes
I'm blind, I'm deaf and now winded as the sharp pain arrows through my ribs
The tip rattling off the bones like stones clinking glass
Grit enters my dry mouth, followed by a funny metallic taste
That forces me to cough disgustedly
I feel thirsty now
I'm trying to move, but for some strange reason I can't
This baffles me as I become frustrated at the lack of communication around me
Hazy shadows dart in and out of my vision, as I start to hear muffled screams
I can still taste metal

Loud noises wake me into reality as I begin to heave violently
My squinting eyes look up urgently from my sandy bed
Lumpy shadow men jump over wooden fences
I think they're running away from the noise, looking back, then forwards
A vice-like grip pinches my skin, hurting me as I let out a gurgled *ouch*
I'm rolled over on to my back
A nose touches mine, a mouth spits in my face,
"Cedric! Cedric!" shouts the voice
This makes me laugh inside of my head,
Who the fuck is Cedric? I wonder
My mouth keeps getting full of liquid metal, I don't like this anymore
I'm trying to talk but I don't know what I'm trying to say?
"Cedric! Cedric!" spits the voice again
I try to tell these people that there is no Cedric
But I can't understand the words that are dribbling out
I think all the noise is stopping now as my vision and hearing are returning
Familiar faces bear down upon mine as they mutter furiously
Looking purposely at me, I try to ask them what the hell they are looking at?
But I don't get an answer
I laugh inside again as their faces remind me of the Three Stooges
I wouldn't be surprised if they started to slap and poke each other!
The voice croaks again as I start to feel to weirdly tired and sleepy, almost floaty
The whirring blades of the incoming helicopter spin the dirty air
Into a tornado of dust, the machine hovering like a giant prehistoric bird
Toying with its prey
My hearing is back to normal thank God
The voice booms again over the raucous bird
Oh fuck, the voice isn't shouting for Cedric… it's calling for the medic.

Dear reader,

We hope you enjoyed reading *Dark Days*. Please take a moment to leave a review in Amazon, even if it's a short one. Your opinion is important to us.

Discover more books by Chris Botragyi at
https://www.nextchapter.pub/authors/chris-botragyi

Want to know when one of our books is free or discounted for Kindle? Join the newsletter at http://eepurl.com/bqqB3H

Best regards,

Chris Botragyi and the Next Chapter Team

You might also like:
Blurred Vision by Chris Botragyi

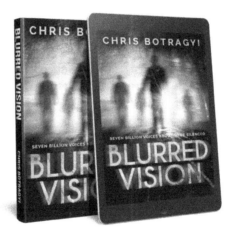

To read the first chapter for free, please head to:
https://www.nextchapter.pub/books/blurred-vision

About the Author

Chris Botragyi was born in 1974, and although originally from Frinton-on-Sea, Essex, he now resides in Westcliff-on-Sea in Southend. As a Learning Support Assistant at a college, Chris works with young adults that suffer from Autism, ADHD, anxieties and mental health illnesses. He is also studying an English Language and Literature degree.

Chris has always been interested in writing. He had a vivid imagination—and still does—at school, and always had a penchant for the paranormal and the macabre. Chris also loves to delve into the human psyche. *Dark Days* demonstrates Chris' foray into poetry, and what drives our darkest desires. Chris says: "I have always had this fascination with the human mind, and what better way to explore this than to combine it with our greatest fears. The results were like nightmares that were then recorded on paper."

As a massive movie and tattoo fan, Chris wrote film and DVD reviews for the *Colchester Circle Online Magazine.* After taking the leap and dabbling with writing two books, he then went on to produce his first science fiction horror novel *Blurred Vision.* Initially six short stories, Chris decided to connect these stories, thus creating the popular novel that it has become today. *Blurred Vision* has gone on to win the Book Reviews Pulp Den Award 2018, and achieved a silver placement at the Ring of Honour Circle Awards 2018.

As a football fanatic, Chris' youth was dominated by watching his beloved Manchester United, as well as local clubs Ipswich Town and Colchester United. He also loves reading, music, art and fashion. "Reading is like acting—it is a way of living somebody else's life without suffering any of the consequences," says Chris.

Lightning Source UK Ltd.
Milton Keynes UK
UKHW041831170521
383897UK00009B/379/J

9 781034 423478